code tales®

Vol 1

Honesty in Emerging Technologies

Nitin Gambhir

Code Tales, Vol 1 : Honesty in Emerging Technologies

First Published 01-01-2025

ISBN: 978-93-342-0926-6
First Edition: January 1, 2025

Self-published by Nitin Gambhir

For permissions, inquiries, or additional information, please contact:
uno.nitin@gmail.com | A704 Saheta CGHS, Plot-30, Sector-4,Dwarka,Delhi 110075.

www.codetales.org

Code Tales, Vol 1: Honesty in Emerging Technologies

Preface for Teens and All Young People

Both my wife and I were raised in joint families. Living with our parents, grand-parents, and extended family members for most of our formative years, we recalled how sitting around the dinner table and listening to the morally uplifting tales and fables from our grand-parents was the charm that made our summers memorable. While we both were trying hard to be hands down parents to our teenage son A, it was the realisation that over-dependence on technology was slowly robbing the current generation of the positive impact moral values can have in shaping their futures.

As per the latest study by Deloitte, nearly 90 percent of leaders of emerging technologies lack the necessary skills to implement ethical principles in development and use. Further, the McKinsey Future of Work study indicates there exists a negative correlation between Ethics and Education. The same study states that 50% of the workforce would need to re-skill by 2025 and prioritizing meta-skills can bridge this gap. As machines learn to advance, humans must also strive to be better but here lies the challenge. Soft-skills are the new Hard-skills.

This struck a chord with me and I decided to go about figuring out the best way to cultivate "human" skills in our young generation. The human skills we collectively need to focus are the abilities to: Problem solve (critical thinking, creativity), Interact with others (collaboration, communication), have global perspectives (curiosity, awareness), be resilient (adaptability, persistence), have impact (initiative, leadership) and most importantly the moral values that we were taught through stories by our parents and teachers during our grown-up years.

The Code Tales book series will help teens and young people to navigate life's challenges while building key skills for their future. Mastering Ethics and Meta-Skills is exactly what they need. Filled with real-life examples, helpful insights, and interactive activities, each volume in the series makes understanding ethics and developing essential life skills fun, approachable, and practical. Storytelling can help illustrate complex ethical concepts. Ethical decision-making is crucial in the development and use of technology and understanding ethics helps teens to become responsible digital citizens.

Be ready to empower yourself as you learn how to make smart, ethical choices in everyday situations. You not only develop critical thinking and problem-solving skills as you learn to code and build a proficiency in computer programming skills but also build self-awareness and confidence to face new challenges. You master skills like adaptability, creativity, and communication on this epic journey towards independence, self-confidence, and a meaningful life.

Standards Addressed:

ISTE Standard for Students 2: Digital Citizen

Students recognize the rights, responsibilities & opportunities of living, learning, and working in an interconnected digital world, act & model in safe, legal, and ethical ways.

Common Core ELA-Literacy.W.4.3

Write narratives to develop real or imagined experiences or events using effective techniques, descriptive details, and clear event sequences.

Table of Contents

Introduction

Code Tales is a classroom-ready resource to empower students to identify and explain key ethical principles and their application to emerging technologies through storytelling, creating digital artefacts, and unplugged activities. Code Tales pedagogy empowers students to gain Digital Literacy and learn meta-skills. An adventure of epic proportions that brings a unique confluence of Life skills and Technology rooted in Ethics.

Meta skills or meta competencies are higher-order cognitive skills such as Creativity, Self-awareness & Resilience that create adaptive learners and act as a key to unlock the development of other technical skills. So as students' progress through their education, it is important to recognize and explore the development of these skills. Alongwith Soft-skills being core to the future of work, Digital Literacy has become mainstream too. It is a common myth that Digital Literacy is the same as Computer Literacy and that the future is only about learning to code. In fact, the three pillars of digital literacy include, (a) finding and consuming digital content, (b) creating digital content, and (c) the ability to share and communicate it effectively.

Code Tales is built for schools to overcome the challenges in teaching meta-skills . The pedagogy is experiential, delivered in hybrid mode, by non-tech teachers and it integrates STEM as it also provides digital literacy.

Inside every Code Tales lesson, the "Moral Bytes" storytelling helps to illustrate complex Ethical concepts in AI as Once upon a time, is resurrected. The "Tech Bytes" introduce a Emerging Technology and its associated Ethical Principles. Finally, "Code Bits" explore a Coding concept that aligns to the ethical tale. With several Digital Artefact Creations the students learn to code and share the game application or animation rooted in Ethics. The Offline Activities reinforce how ethical principles shape technology use with several unplugged activities including quick board games, presentations, designing campaigns for school etc.

The key objective is that students can identify and explain key ethical principles and their application to emerging technologies through storytelling and practical examples. Ethical principles are fundamental guidelines for moral behavior. Emerging technologies present new ethical challenges and opportunities. Ethical decision-making is crucial in the development and use of technology. Understanding ethics helps us become responsible digital citizens.

vol 1

Honesty and Transparency

Moral Bytes

Honesty and Transparency - Ethical principles in Emerging technologies

In this strand, the focus will be on truthfulness in digital communications and the importance of credibility in online interactions. Ethics are the rules that help us decide what is right and wrong. Just like we have rules for playing games, we need rules for using technology.

The concept of honesty in the digital age can be related to the story of "The Fox and the Crow." This tale teaches us that lying, even online, can have serious consequences. As we explore social media and messaging apps, we will discover how important it is to be truthful in our digital interactions, how false information spreads online, and its potential consequences.

When sharing information digitally, responsible online communication is the key. To prevent spread of misinformation online, fact-checking is critical, especially now when "fake news" is becoming a menace with the onset of Generative AI. One should be aware about digital reputation and how honesty in online interactions affects it. The story's moral applies to online behavior, particularly in social media contexts. Honesty also applies in civic engagement and media. Companies should be like good friends – honest about what they do and do not do. They should explain how they use our information and the risks associated with their products. This is called transparency, and it is super important in building trust. Transparency in government and businesses and how technology can promote or hinder transparency should be made central to all decision making.

The Fox and the Crow

If someone flatters you, think hard before trusting them.

The Truth Behind the Screen: Honesty in the Digital Age

In emerging technologies, honesty and transparency are as important in Aesop's fable of the Fox and the Crow. Just as the fox used flattery to trick the crow into dropping its cheese, some technologies might use clever tactics to get what they want from us – our data, attention, or money. Imagine social media as the fox, always telling us how great we look or how interesting our lives are. Like the crow, we might puff up with pride and share more and more information. But what if, like the fox's true intentions, these platforms aren't always honest about using our data? New technologies like artificial intelligence and virtual reality are exciting but tricky. AI might seem super smart, like the flattering fox, but it is important to remember that it can make mistakes or be biased. Virtual reality can show us amazing worlds, but we should be careful not to lose touch with the real one, just as the crow lost its cheese by believing the fox's lies. As users, we should not be likewise crows, not easily fooled by flattery or fancy features.

We should ask questions, read terms of service (even though they are boring!), and think critically about how we use technology. In the end, the clever fox got the cheese, but the crow learned a valuable lesson. Similarly, by valuing honesty and transparency in our digital world, we can enjoy the benefits of new technologies while staying safe and informed. Remember, it is important to look beyond sweet words to find the truth.

Tech Bytes

"How and why the ethical principles of Honesty and Transparency apply to Emerging technologies"

In the digital age, honesty and transparency have taken on new dimensions. As our lives become increasingly intertwined with technology, the importance of truthful communication and open disclosure of information has never been more critical. Understanding these principles is fundamental to becoming responsible digital citizens.

Honesty in the online world extends beyond simply telling the truth. It encompasses the integrity of the information we share, the authenticity of our online personas, and the transparency of our digital interactions. In an era where misinformation can spread at the click of a button, value honesty is crucial.

This includes understanding the consequences of sharing false information, the importance of fact-checking, and the responsibility that comes with having a digital voice. Emerging technologies like social media platforms and instant messaging apps have made communication faster and more accessible than ever before. However, they have also created new challenges for maintaining honesty and transparency. What we share online can have real-world consequences, affecting our relationships, reputation, and even future opportunities.

Smart Home Devices and Transparency

Transparency is the ethical principle of being open, clear, and honest about one's actions and intentions. Smart home devices, such as voice-activated assistants, smart thermostats, and security cameras, are becoming increasingly common in our homes. These devices collect and process vast amounts of data about our daily lives to provide personalized services and improve our living environments. However, the way these devices operate and use our data is not always clear to users. For instance, voice-activated assistants may be listening even when we are not actively using them, and smart thermostats may be sharing our energy usage data with third parties. This lack of transparency can lead to privacy concerns and mistrust in technology.

By fostering an understanding of transparency in smart home technologies, we can become more informed and empowered users of the devices. This knowledge will be crucial as smart home technologies continue to evolve and become more integrated into our daily lives.

To address these issues, technology companies are working on providing clearer information about data collection practices, giving users more control over their data, and making it easier to understand how AI-powered devices make decisions. Thus, it is important to understand the timeless value of honesty and its modern applications.

Code Bits

The concept of Sequence in Programming and the Ethical tale

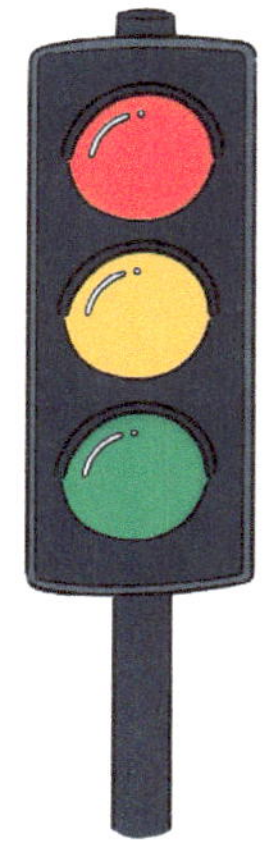

Sequence simply means, the order in which the set of instructions are to be performed to complete a task. The Fox and Crow tale follows a sequence: the crow has cheese, the fox sees it, and flatters the crow, the crow opens its beak to sing, and the cheese falls. A common way to know the order of an instruction is by using numbered steps or putting them in consecutive lines (top to bottom). Most common way to create a sequence is by following them from top to bottom. The next instruction followed only after completing previous instruction. Like in a relay race, one member is running at a time. Once he completes, "the baton" is passed to the next member. Sequencing is like a relay on a long straight track, with the runners lined up in a straight line.

Real-life is full of Sequences. Lights! Camera! Action! Movie directors give instructions to crew members and actors all the time which are sequential.

"Look what I created!" While doing craft work with glue-stick you follow a sequence. Step 1: Clean the surfaces. Step 2: Apply a thin layer of glue on any surface. Step 3: Spread the glue evenly. Step 4: Press the surfaces together. Step 5: Leave them for 10 minutes.

"Stars, hide your fires" A theatrical play like 'Macbeth' too has a sequence in every act. Guess, Shakespeare was an early programmer too!

Some technologies have a sequence to collect user data. Technology companies should be transparent about data collection. They should clearly explain what data will be collected and describe how data will be used. They should ask for explicit consent to collect the data and use it only as agreed.

Step 1: The user signs up and agrees to terms (often without reading).
Step 2: The user interacts with the platform.
Step 3: The Platform collects data and uses or sells it.

Users can follow a sequence to protect themselves. Firstly, read the terms of service and understand data usage policies. Make informed decisions about sharing and regularly review privacy settings. Keep monitoring account activity.

Unplugged Activities

These offline activities are designed to understand how sequences work in storytelling and coding. Students will also gain valuable insight into how technology companies might use sequences to collect data. They will also discuss creating a sequence of actions to stay safe online.

Activity # 1:

Create a "Truth vs. Fiction" bulletin board where students post examples of true and false information, they find online.

Activity # 2:

Role-play scenarios involving honest and dishonest online behavior, discussing the outcomes of each.

Activity # 3:

Students create a simple flowchart or sequence diagram that shows: Sequence of events in the fox and crow story, parallel sequence of how a social media platform collects & uses data and the steps users can take to protect their privacy online

Virtual Adaptation:

Share news articles or stories via screen share. Students can use reaction buttons or the chat feature to vote on whether they think each story is fact or fiction.

Stretch Goal:

Design an "Honesty in Tech" campaign for the school.

Lesson Assessment:

Students create a digital poster explaining the importance of honesty in online communication.

Offline Game

Coder's Gig : A 2 player game of logical reasoning

Step 1:
Make 9 (Nine) playing cards, one for each of the words shown below. Cut them out to play.

Step 2:
Place the cards face –up and toss a coin to choose who goes first !

Directions and Rules of the Game:
Each player takes turn to pick up a card.
To win you must get all the cards that have the same letter.

For example, if you picked up TICK, TOK, TAN, you would win as you have all cards containing letter T

If all cards are taken with no one having all particular letter, then the game is a draw.

TICK	TOK	CAN	PIN	OK
DIP	COD	PAD	TAN	

Introduction to the Scratch3.0 coding platform

Scratch3.0 Offline version - Steps to download

Please follow the steps mentioned below to access the coding platform to enable the student to start creating applications

Step 1:
Use the link below:
Scratch - Scratch Offline Editor (https://scratch.mit.edu)

Step 2:
Please download the compatible offline version of Scratch programming software based on the Operating System for your laptop (Windows/Mac OS)
for Windows 10 / Mac OS, download the Scratch offline editor app.

Alternatively for older versions of Windows you can download the Scratch 2 . 0 offline editor. This will help to access the coding platform without an active internet connection. You can use the link below and type it in your internet browser:
Scratch - Scratch 2.0 (https://scratch.mit.edu/download/scratch2)

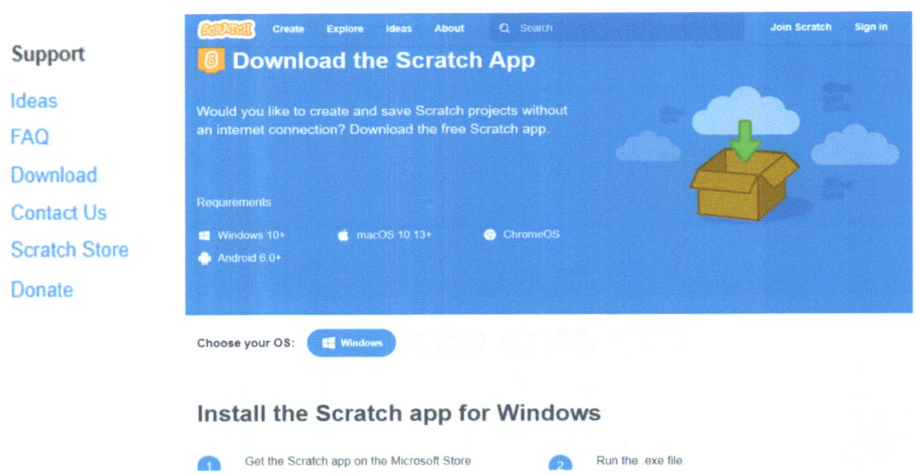

In case of any issues or queries regarding the installation, please do not hesitate to contact us at **sayhello@stemmetaverse.io**

Since you might not have active internet all the time, it is advisable to download the offline editor.

Scratch3.0 Online version - Steps to Register & Sign-in

Please follow the steps mentioned below to access the coding platform to enable the student to start creating applications online.

In addition to the Offline version, the student can also create the game applications by using the online version on any PC / Laptop with an active good internet connection.

Step 1:
Visit Scratch - Imagine, Program, Share (https://scratch.mit.edu)

Step 2:
Click 'Join' and create a Username & Password for the website. Please keep a safe record of the same for all future login.

Step 3:
Once registered and account is created, click 'Create' on the top ribbon of the webpage.

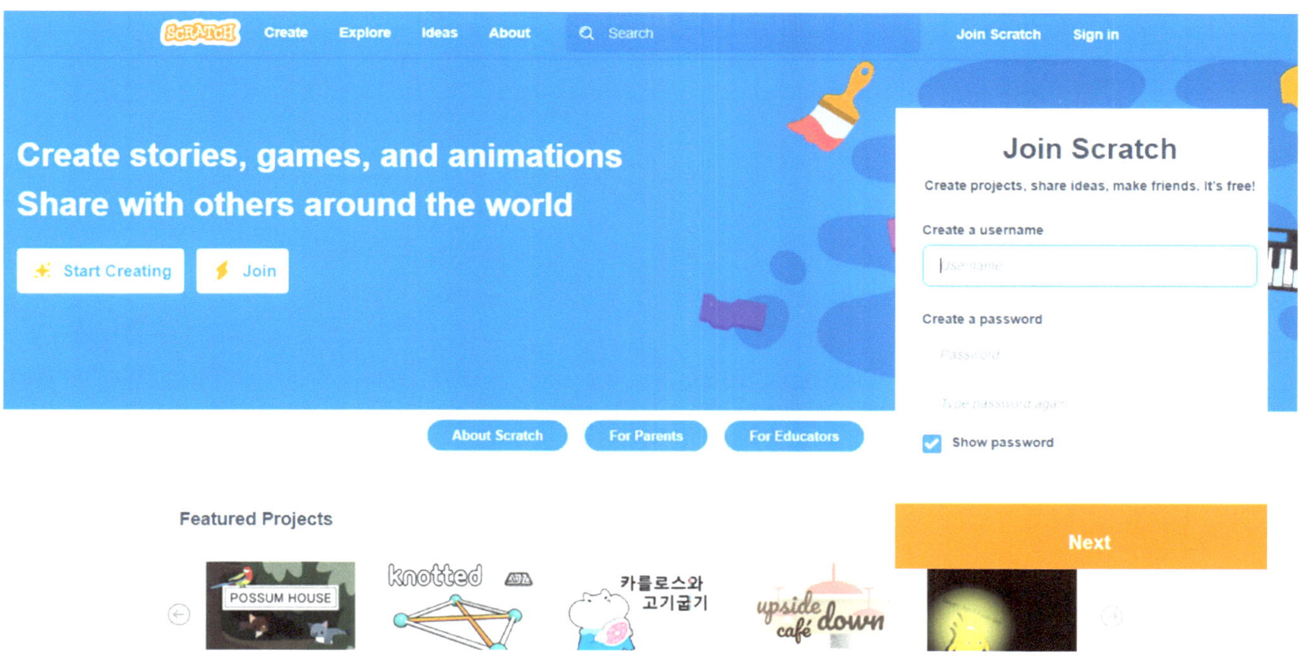

Scratch3.0 - Coding Platform

Code

Coding blocks can be used to control your sprites and stage. All blocks are color coded and bundled together as categories.Adding any Code block is simple -Select - Drag - Drop

Stage

This is the section where your sprites / actors perform the output as per your Code Instructions. You can change the background of your stage by clicking any of these options.

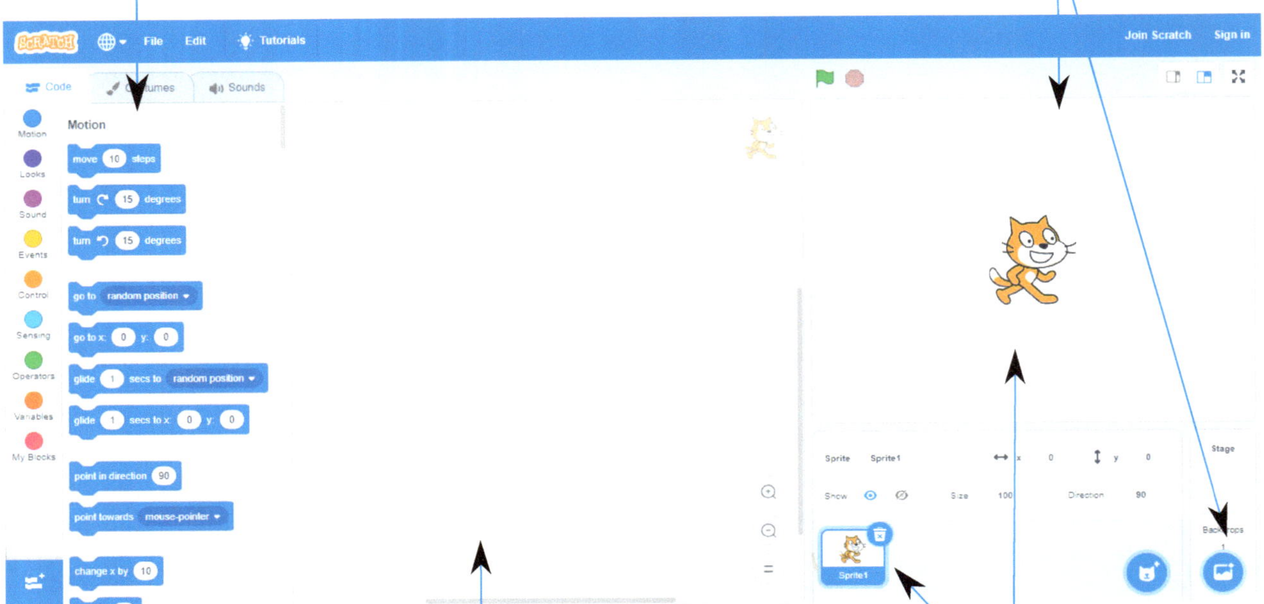

Script

Code blocks are dragged and dropped into this section to create an instruction for the Sprite.Code blocks stick to each other like magnets. Each Sprite and background has its own Script area

Sprite

These are just like actors for your game or story animation. Code each individual sprite to perform as per your logic. You can have any number of sprites in your program

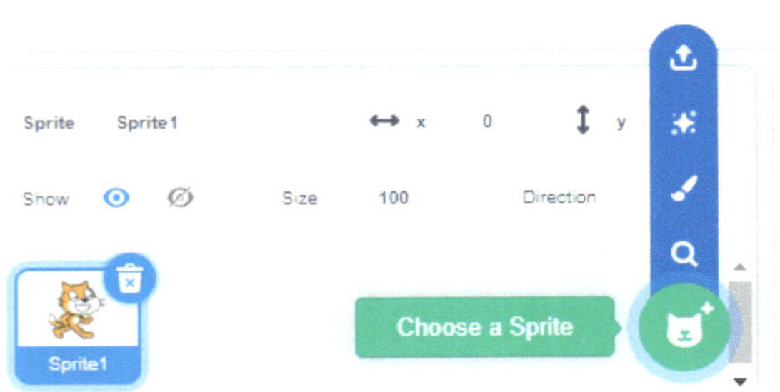

Options to Add New Sprite

1. Upload your own Image Sprite
2. Get a Random surprise Sprite
3. Paint your own Sprite
4. Select a Sprite from in-built library

Download the Game Template

Step 1:
Open any web-browser like Google Chrome etc. and type-in the shortened URL link written in the Step 1 of the Code Card Page. This will open the Game Project on the MIT Scratch website.

Step 2:
Click the "See Inside" blue button to open the Game Template on the Online Scratch Editor.

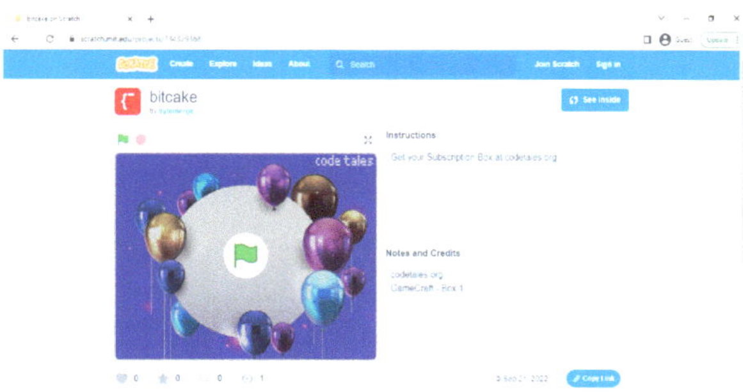

Step 3:
Click the "Sign In" blue button to login into your MIT Scratch Online account.

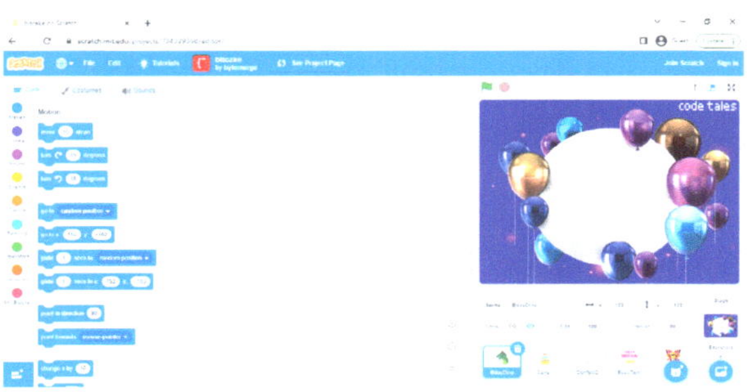

Step 4:
Once logged-in to your account, click the green "Remix" button on top and you are ready to build your code using the given Code Cards.

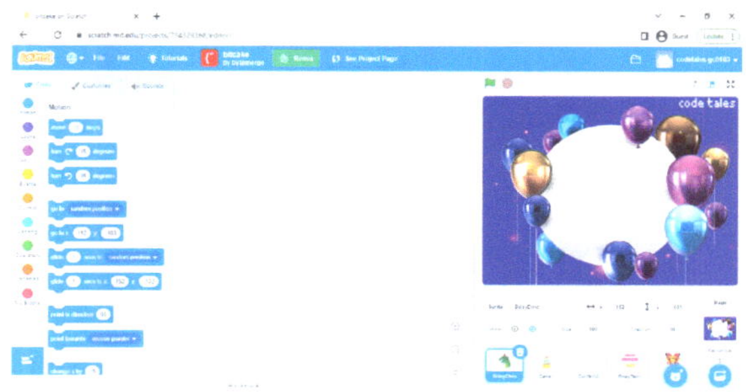

Step 5:
Once you have made the complete game, click on the "File" tab and select "Save to your computer" option to download your game.

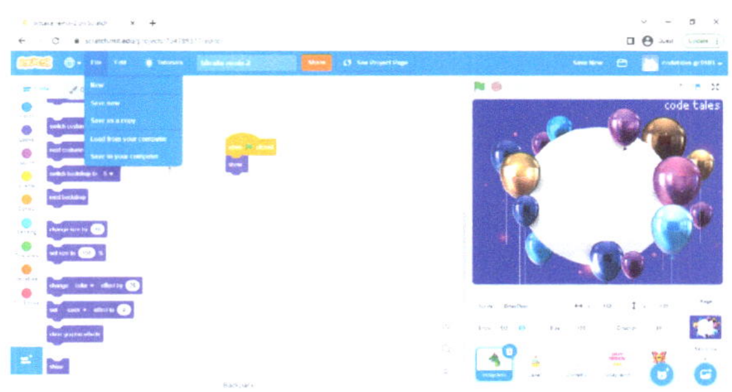

Bonus #1
Birthday
Card

Step 1:

Get Scratch template

https://bit.ly/3BZpUgJ

Step 2:

Create the Code blocks for each Sprite of your game app using the instructions given in next page.

Each sprite has it's own set of instructions that are created by using the code blocks attached to form a sequence to give an output.

Script for Birthday Card

Script for Background

```
when [flag] clicked
wait (1) seconds
switch backdropto (1 ▾)
play sound (birthday ▾) until done
```

Script for Cake sprite

```
when [flag] clicked
hide
```

```
when backdropswitchesto (1 ▾)
wait (3) seconds
show
go tox: (7) y: (-1)
```

Script for Birthday Text sprite

```
when [flag] clicked
hide
```

```
when backdropswitchesto (1 ▾)
wait (7) seconds
show
go tox: (-135) y: (83)
```

Script for Bday Dino sprite

```
when [flag] clicked
hide
```

```
when backdropswitchesto (1 ▾)
wait (1) seconds
show
go tox: (152) y: (-103)
```

Script for Confetti sprite

```
when [flag] clicked
hide
```

```
when backdropswitchesto (1 ▾)
wait (9) seconds
show
go tox: (-4) y: (-7)
```

Script for Gift sprite

```
when [flag] clicked
hide
```

```
when backdropswitchesto (1 ▾)
wait (5) seconds
show
go tox: (-159) y: (-113)
```

Bonus #2
Knock Knock

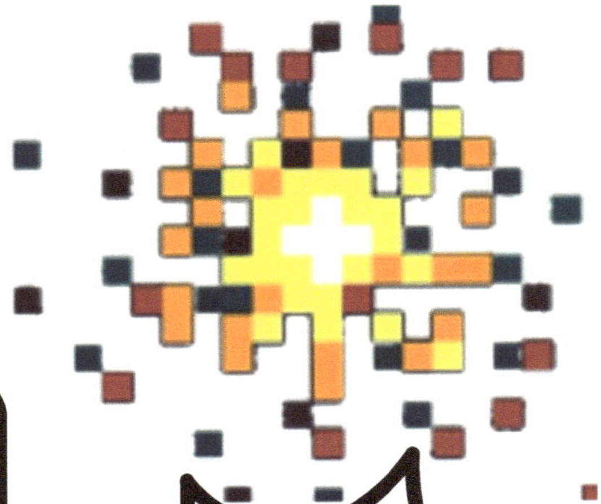

Step 1:

Get Scratch template

https://bit.ly/3LuShpU

Step 2:

Create the Code blocks for each Sprite of your game app using the instructions given in next page.

Each sprite has it's own set of instructions that are created by using the code blocks attached to form a sequence to give an output.

Script for Knock Knock

Script for Boy on the left

```
when [flag] clicked
hide
```

```
when backdropswitchesto 2 ▾
show
wait 2 seconds
say Knock Knock! for 2 seconds
wait 4 seconds
say Coco for 2 seconds
wait 4 seconds
say Cocoh nut! for 2 seconds
wait 1 seconds
say hahaha! for 2 seconds
```

Script for Boy on the right

```
when [flag] clicked
hide
```

```
when backdropswitchesto 2 ▾
show
wait 5 seconds
say Who's there? for 2 seconds
wait 4 seconds
say Coco who? for 2 seconds
wait 4 seconds
say Lol! for 2 seconds
```

Script for Background

```
when [flag] clicked
switch backdropto 1 ▾
play sound xylo4 ▾ until done
switch backdropto 2 ▾
play sound dance chillout ▾ until done
wait 9 seconds
play sound clapping ▾ until done
```

Bonus #3
Water Cycle

Step 1:

Get Scratch template

https://bit.ly/3LCQwY4

Step 2:

Create the Code blocks for each Sprite of your game app using the instructions given in next page.

Each sprite has it's own set of instructions that are created by using the code blocks attached to form a sequence to give an output.

Script for Water Cycle

Script for Sun sprite

```
when [flag] clicked
go to x: 192 y: 133
set ghost effect to 100
wait 1 seconds
set ghost effect to 50
wait 1 seconds
set ghost effect to 0
wait 1 seconds
```

Script for Water vapor sprite

```
when [flag] clicked
go to x: 172 y: -42
set ghost effect to 100
wait 3 seconds
set ghost effect to 0
glide 2 secs to x: 172 y: 28
wait 0.5 seconds
set ghost effect to 50
wait 0.5 seconds
set ghost effect to 100
```

Script for Cloud sprite

```
when [flag] clicked
go to x: 147 y: 73
set ghost effect to 100
wait 5 seconds
set ghost effect to 75
wait 1 seconds
set ghost effect to 0
glide 5 secs to x: -125 y: 73
wait 1 seconds
set ghost effect to 50
```

Script for Rain clouds sprite

```
when [flag] clicked
go to x: -125 y: 50
set ghost effect to 100
wait 11 seconds
set ghost effect to 50
wait 1 seconds
set ghost effect to 0
```

Script for River flowing sprite

```
when [flag] clicked
go to x: -136 y: -44
set ghost effect to 90
wait 12 seconds
set ghost effect to 75
wait 2 seconds
set ghost effect to 50
wait 1 seconds
set ghost effect to 0
wait 1 seconds
glide 5 secs to x: -100 y: -60
```

Mega Bytes Merge-The Fox and the Crow

Flowcharts help to plan a scene from our story. Each step is shown as a box with an arrow leading to the next step. (Sometimes boxes can be questions so can have more arrows with it.)

Each step follows another in a specific order to achieve the desired outcome.

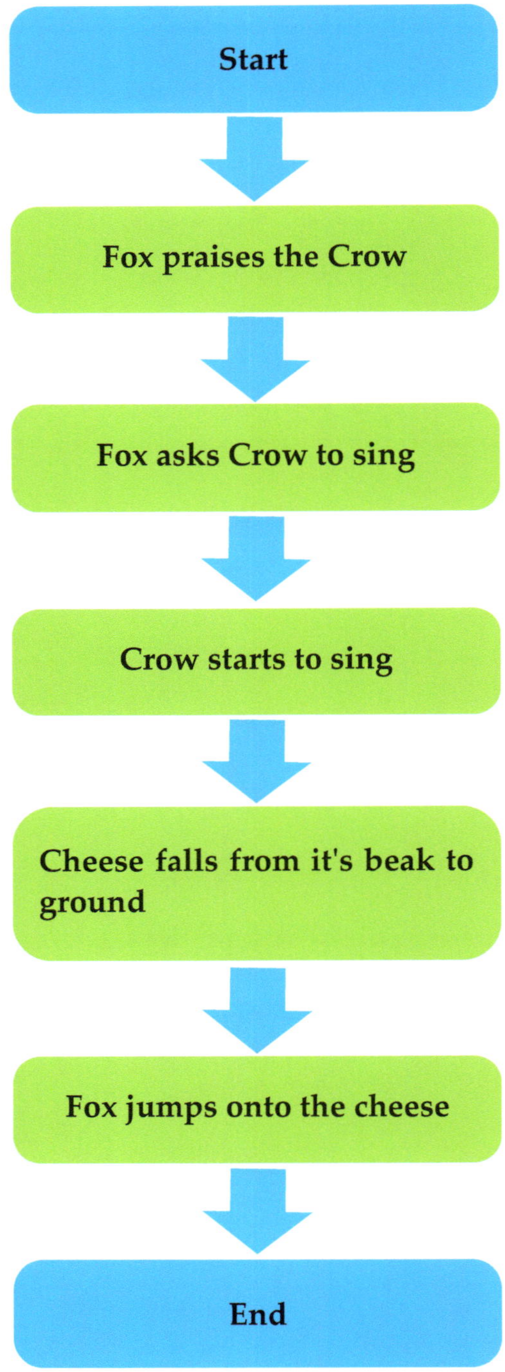

Computers need instructions given in their language to perform our tasks. Algorithms are written set of instructions & consist of:

1. actions to be taken

2. order they must be done in

Online Activity

The Fox and the Crow

Step 1:

Get Scratch template

https://bit.ly/3BAuXTa

Step 2:

Create the Code blocks for each Sprite of your game app using the instructions given in next page.

Remember Merge MB
Do check the flowchart for creating the animation

Each sprite has it's own set of instructions that are created by using the code blocks attached to form a sequence to give an output.

Script for The Fox and the Crow

Script for Crow sprite

```
when 🏁 clicked
hide
```

```
when backdropswitchesto 3 ▾
hide
```

```
when backdropswitchesto Forest ▾
show
go tox: 127 y: 98
switch costumeto Sitting ▾
wait 7 seconds
say Yes Icansing! for 2 seconds
start sound bird ▾
switch costumeto Singing ▾
```

Script for Background

```
when 🏁 clicked
switch backdropto 1 ▾
wait 2 seconds
switch backdropto Forest ▾
wait 15 seconds
switch backdropto 3 ▾
```

Script for Fox sprite

```
when 🏁 clicked
hide
```

```
when backdropswitchesto 3 ▾
hide
```

```
when backdropswitchesto Forest ▾
show
switch costumeto Praising ▾
wait 2 seconds
say Oh!beautiful bird for 2 seconds
switch costumeto Questioning ▾
wait 1 seconds
say If onlyyoucouldsing? for 2 seconds
wait 5 seconds
switch costumeto Jumping ▾
```

Script for Cheese sprite

```
when 🏁 clicked
hide
```

```
when backdropswitchesto 3 ▾
hide
```

```
when backdropswitchesto Forest ▾
show
go tox: 79 y: 109
wait 10 seconds
glide 2 secs tox: 79 y: -160
```

Flash Cards

function	1	A piece of code that you can call again and again and has a specific task to perform always	1
bit	2	A bit is single unit of information in a computer, usually represented by 0 or 1.	2
input	3	Way to give information to a computer	3
binary	4	A way of representing information using only two options.	4
output	5	Way to get information out of a computer	5
conditionals	6	instructions that run only when some condition is met	6
search engine	7	A program that searches a database for keywords or characters as given by a user among the sites on the world wide web	7
cyber-bullying	10	Treating another person on the internet badly and making them feel angry,sad or scared with your actions	10
repeat	9	to do something again and again	9
data	12	Data is information which can be either in form of integers, floats,text or symbols that are input or output of a program	12

Curriculum Overview

Code Tales is a learner-centric resource built to overcome the challenges in teaching meta-skills. The pedagogy is experiential, delivered in hybrid mode, by non-tech teachers and it integrates STEM.

Strand 1
Vol 1: Honesty and Transparency
Focus on truthfulness in digital communications and the importance of credibility.
Vol 2: Empathy and Kindness
Focusing on positive contributions to online communities and digital collaboration.
Vol 3: Responsibility and Accountability
Ownership of one's digital actions and working together in online environments.

Strand 2
Vol 4: Privacy and Security
Importance of safeguarding personal information and understanding data collection.
Vol 5: Environmental Stewardship and Sustainability
Responsibility to consider the environmental impact of technology use.
Vol 6: Fairness and Equality
Addressing the need for unbiased decision-making and equal treatment of all users.

Strand 3
Vol 7: Collaboration and Teamwork
Applying ethical principles to create positive change in the digital world.
Vol 8: Respect for Intellectual Property
Explore the ethical use of creative technologies and respect others' digital creations.
Vol 9: Critical Thinking and Information Literacy
Importance of maintaining security and being trustworthy in digital interactions.
Vol 10: Creativity and Innovation
Address the need to design technology accessible to all users, regardless of abilities.

www.ingramcontent.com/pod-product-compliance
Lightning Source LLC
Chambersburg PA
CBHW041528180726
48282CB00053B/113